HOW TO IMPROVE YOUR CONFIDENCE

DR KENNETH HAMBLY grew up and trained as a doctor in Northern Ireland, and has since worked in Canada and in England and Scotland. He has practised as a gynaecologist and a general practitioner, and currently works in Ayrshire. He has also written *Overcoming Tension*, *The Nervous Person's Companion* and *Coping Successfully With Agoraphobia* for Sheldon Press.

Overcoming Common Problems Series

For a full list of titles please contact
Sheldon Press, Marylebone Road, London NW1 4DU

Overcoming Common Problems Series

Overcoming Common Problems Series

Overcoming Common Problems

HOW TO IMPROVE
YOUR CONFIDENCE

Dr Kenneth Hambly

M.B., B.Ch., M.R.C.O.G.

SHELDON PRESS
LONDON

First published in Great Britain in 1987 by
Sheldon Press, SPCK, Marylebone Road, London NW1 4DU

Seventh impression 1994

British Library Cataloguing in Publication Data

Hambly, Kenneth
    How to improve your confidence. –
    (Overcoming common problems).
    1. Self-confidence
    I. Title   II. Series
    158'.1   BF575-S/

ISBN 0-85969-563-8

Printed in England by Clays Ltd, St Ives plc

For my wife, Alison

Contents

Introduction

As a family doctor I see patients with many problems. Not all of these are purely medical. Patients also come with all sorts of emotional, psychological and social difficulties. Often there are parts of their lives which are unsatisfactory and with which they need help. There is often one problem which causes continuing distress and disruption and which seems to intrude into every aspect of an individual's life – a lack of confidence. People think that if they could improve their self-confidence, their relationships with others would be better, their work would be easier, and their entire lives more fulfilled.

Perhaps this is the one part of our lives we would all like to see improved. After all, no-one always feels completely at ease all of the time. No-one is always relaxed. For some people, that can be a minor discomfort, but for others it can be a cause of great distress and embarrassment. It can ruin their lives. But does it need to?

Confidence *can* be improved. We can all learn to be more confident, to 'gain in confidence'. If you ever feel that *you* are lacking in confidence, then this book has been written for you.

Some people are born confident. Others are born not so confident, and for them the world can be a hostile and difficult place. Some people who have always considered themselves to be confident have suddenly found that they are not as confident as they thought. Confidence can be lost after some unpleasant event such as a divorce or perhaps a psychiatric illness or sudden unemployment. There are many events in this life which can make us lose confidence in ourselves.

Confidence is not always the same. At different times, we feel confident or we may not, there are situations in which we are confident and situations in which we are not. Confidence can be elusive. And yet we are surrounded by confident people, or rather by people who *seem* to be confident. In our society it is a much prized attribute. If we are in business we are supposed to exude confidence. If we are teachers we need confidence if we are to stand in front of a class. No matter what our occupation, no matter where we live, we are expected to have confidence. Our society has almost made it into a cult. No doubt much of the popularity of James Bond is due to his total command of every situation and the obvious confidence he displays at all times.

We need confidence, but can we really improve on our self-confidence? Can we really make our lives more enjoyable, or is that just an unattainable dream?

Confidence *can* be improved. We *can* learn to be more confident. But we have to go about it the right way, we have to work at it. We have to make an effort, and if that effort is well-directed we can make tremendous improvements in our confidence and thus in our sense of well-being. We can get more enjoyment out of our lives, more fulfilment, more pleasure. That is worth working for.

In the following pages I will show you ways of improving your confidence. I will help you to help yourself. There is no need for you to feel uncomfortable, isolated and alone for much of your life. We all have great resources we often don't fully use. If you feel that you are sometimes lacking in confidence it is time you did something about it. Why not start now?

1
What is Confidence?

Most people would admit that they would like to be more confident, more at ease with themselves. So what *is* this elusive thing we call confidence? We all have an idea of what we mean when we talk about it. The dictionary describes confidence as 'boldness', but that somehow doesn't seem to be quite right. It isn't boldness we are seeking. Self-assurance seems to be more like it. We want to be able to handle or be comfortable in any situation.

Confidence has a lot to do with our relationships with other people. We don't want to feel inferior to anyone. We don't want to be bullied by anyone. We would like to be the boy who can walk up to any girl and ask her for a date, or the girl who can wear anything she wants to wear and still feel good because she knows that her judgement is right. We want to be able to walk into any roomful of people and feel that we *are* just as good as any of them – and know that we *are* just as good as any of them.

When we go to work, we want to fulfil our potential and not be held back by any feelings of inferiority. We want to be able to go to meetings and contribute as much as anyone else. We would like to feel at ease with ourselves, our workmates and the public if dealing with the public is part of our job.

If we go to a party or to any social event we want to enjoy ourselves, without embarrassment. We want self-assurance and self-reliance. We want to feel *confident*.

Perhaps this is all very obvious. Of course we all want these things. Yet wanting something and having it is very different. And if not all of us have confidence, if we haven't been born with an abundance of it, we must set about obtaining some.

3

Who Needs Confidence?

Let me introduce you to some people whom I have got to know very well.

Mrs McD.

Mrs McD had been coming to see me regularly for some months. She was in her forties, attractive and she had a family of two girls. She had done office work, but when she had her family she stayed at home to look after them. She managed very well. She was a pleasant outgoing individual, generally well-liked. So why was she attending her doctor?

She had developed a problem. Several months previously she had begun to feel anxious from time to time. At first she had ignored it, but the feeling became worse until it really began to bother her. That is when she came to see me. She wasn't sure whether I would be able to help or not, but she felt that she had to talk to someone.

I was able to help her and she began to feel better. She became more at ease with herself, and we both thought that her problems were over.

'Why don't you think about going back to work?' I asked her one day when she came to the surgery.

'Work?' she replied. 'I couldn't work now. I might have been able to before this illness, but not now. I couldn't even consider it.'

'Why not?' I asked.

'Why not? My confidence is shattered, that's why. I don't think I will ever be able to work again. I really don't. I just couldn't face people. I feel uneasy in groups of people, and then I've always had to work with the public and I just couldn't do that. No, I think my working days are over.'

Mrs McD had quite simply lost confidence in herself. She really did want to go back to work, and this would have helped her, but she felt that she couldn't manage it.

Mr J.C.

Mr J.C. was a well-known local businessman, a tall, slightly obese man in his early fifties. He had called to see me one day, and we were having a cup of coffee together. He mentioned that he had been elected captain of the local golf club. I congratulated him.

'Thank you very much', he replied. 'I hope I can manage it.'

'Why wouldn't you manage it?' I asked, surprised.

'Ah, well. There's a lot of speech-making and that sort of thing,' he said.

'Does that bother you?' I asked.

'Well, yes it does. I'm afraid I'm not very confident about these things. I get very nervous. I used to be able to do anything, but not any more. I don't know why. I just seem to have lost confidence. Is there anything you can do to help me?'

Peter F.

Peter was in his late teens, the son of a friend of mine. I knew him well and had always liked him and thought of him as an outgoing sort of young man, obliging and able. He came to see me in my surgery one day, and surprisingly told me that he was extremely unhappy. He was having all sorts of problems and was in despair. We talked for a long time and at the end of the day it seemed that his problems boiled down to one thing. Peter was excruciatingly shy.

'I'm shy with girls,' he explained. 'I just don't seem to be able to get on with them. I am just too shy to even approach a girl. No-one else seems to have this problem. I really just don't know what to do. I don't know if there is anything you can do to help?'

So Peter had a similar problem to the others. His was shyness – a lack of confidence in himself in dealings with the opposite sex. That is something which afflicts many young people of both sexes. And it isn't a joke. It can make adolescence very miserable indeed. It takes a lot of courage to

5

discuss these personal matters with a stranger, even if the stranger is a doctor who should know of ways to help. In their own different ways, these people were desperate. And they aren't the only ones. The world is full of people who feel that they are lacking in confidence in one or more areas of their lives, and would like to improve things. Nothing in this life is fixed. Personality is dynamic, and capable of change, so we can always improve if we go about it the right way.

You may have noticed that the three people I introduced you to are very different, and that they have different problems. They certainly wouldn't see their problems as being the same, and in a way they are not. But they are all caused by the same thing – a lack of confidence. It may affect them in different ways, but the basic cause is the same. If that problem could be solved, then each of them would be able to live happier and more fulfilled lives.

The Problem

The problem is to overcome this lack of confidence. But before we can do that we have to sort out a few things. First, we have to decide if we really want to change things? After all, we don't *have* to do anything. A little shyness can be an attractive thing. Brashness certainly isn't attractive. But suppose that this lack of confidence is causing real problems in our work or in our social or family lives?

Suppose we really don't like the way we are, just how far are we prepared to go to change things? How far can we go and what can be achieved? You can see that the three people mentioned above might have different problems and different goals, but the solution and the techniques they must use are essentially the same. That is because behind each of their problems is this lack of confidence.

We have all heard a sports commentator say, 'This young

man is going from strength to strength. He is gaining in confidence every day.' Or a political observer might say, 'Mr Jones is more impressive each time he speaks. He is gaining in confidence all the time.' It is accepted that confidence can be improved. It is also accepted that even very influential and important people may be lacking in confidence at the beginning of a job, but that they will get better with experience, just as the sportsman will gain in stature with experience and the passage of time.

The Task

We have a job to do. It may just be being the captain of the golf club, or it may be that our task is living life to the full. First we have to decide just what we want to achieve, then how we are going to achieve it.

What do we want to achieve?

It is decision time. We must make a start. So what sort of changes do we really want to make in our lives? Remember that we can't change our *basic* personalities. We are who we are. We can't change and I doubt if many people would want to. We just can't become someone else in personality any more than we can suddenly look like someone else. But we can improve what we have got, just as we can improve our appearance.

We must have a goal, and it should be an attainable goal. That goal might be different for each of us. We are probably all confident in at least one area of our lives. In what other areas do we want to achieve confidence? And there is no point in saying that we want to play football for England, or be prime minister. Let us set simple attainable goals. We can always move on to more ambitious goals later.

Let's go back to the individuals we met earlier. Mrs McD's problem was that she wanted to go back to work but she felt she hadn't got the confidence. That wasn't her only problem, of course. I knew that there were many things she would have liked to have been able to do, but which she avoided doing because she was lacking in confidence. She avoided shopping in supermarkets, for example – she didn't like crowded places. But what she most wanted to do was to be able to go back to work. So that is what we set out to achieve.

Mr J.C. was a businessman, competent and able. No one would ever have thought him to be lacking in confidence, but in one small area he was. He didn't like public speaking, didn't feel confident about it. This was going to spoil his year as captain of the golf club. Maybe this would not be too important a thing to many people, but it was to him. He had wanted to be captain for many years and this lack of confidence was going to ruin his year. He really did want to be a success, but there was that dreaded feeling that he might have to make speeches and that he would make a mess of it. He might break down in public. He might not be able to speak the words. His ambition was simply to be able to speak in public with confidence.

Peter had his whole life in front of him. He had those critical years of courtship and marriage to come, and he was missing out. Not only that, he wasn't having any fun, and at his age he should have been having a ball. A lack of confidence was so serious for him that he was in despair. He wanted urgent help in order to get on with his life. He couldn't do that unless he found some confidence somewhere.

All these people had realistic expectations. They knew what they wanted and they were prepared to work to achieve their ambitions. So do you know what you want and are you prepared to work to achieve it? If you are, how do you go about it? How do you achieve confidence? It's not easy. There is absolutely no point in just saying to yourself, 'I will be confident. I can and I will.' You can't and you won't, and it will be demoralizing. You can't control your thoughts any more than you can change who you are.

There has to be another way of going about it, and fortunately there is – the way of common sense. There are no tricks or short cuts, only common sense and hard work, and with help you would be surprised just how much you can achieve in a short time.

You have many resources within yourself that you don't fully use. We all have. We don't do ourselves justice, and we know it. We are all more able and more competent than we appear to be.

I would ask you to have confidence in one thing. Have confidence that you *can* improve your self-confidence. Make that an act of faith. Believe that you *can* do it, and you will.

2

Why Aren't We Confident?

Before we go any further it is worth taking a little more time to consider our problem in a little more detail. If we can't sort out the real nature of the problem we have no chance of finding a cure.

What's causing our lack of confidence?

Perhaps its just the way we are. Perhaps some of us just aren't born confident. Perhaps it's just a cross we have to bear. That might be the view that some people take, but I don't think it is correct. Let us try an experiment. Sit in a comfortable chair and think of the situation which makes you feel least confident. Imagine that you are *in* that situation. Picture it in your mind's eye. Really work at it. Now think, 'How do I feel?' Try to note just how you feel physically. What is your pulse doing? Do you feel sick? Are you sweating?

Physical reactions

If you have any imagination at all you might just notice that you don't feel very well. You will have developed real physical symptoms just by imagining yourself in that difficult situation. This is not unusual. Remember Mr J.C.? His problem was that he lacked confidence in his ability to make speeches in public. In other ways he was fine. But why did he fear that particular situation? He was certainly as good a speaker as anyone else and better than most. His problem was that when he stood up to speak he felt sick, shaky and ill. No wonder he worried about it.

Furthermore, Mr J.C. knew that if he even thought about making a speech, he would feel just the same way. In fact, sometimes thinking about a speech was worse than actually making it. The anticipation could be worse than the event.

The same was true of Peter. It was almost as if he was allergic to girls. If he was to approach one he would feel ill. And in a way he *was* allergic to girls. He had a 'psychological allergy'.

In Mrs McD.'s case work was her problem, and she would feel shaky and a little sick if she imagined herself in the actual situation she would have to face at work. She had a real physical reaction to that situation.

If a situation makes someone feel ill, he or she is not going to have a sense of confidence. Confidence is a word we use to describe a state of mind without really saying what we mean. You could describe yourself as 'not being a very confident person'. That might be your personality type. But what you are saying is 'I am the sort of person who isn't very comfortable in many situations.' That is the same as saying that you are the sort of person who has unpleasant physical sensations in many common situations. Confidence may well be a state of mind, but it also has a physical side. That is why simply telling yourself that you are getting better and better will do absolutely no good. You have to consider the whole problem.

I hope we are now beginning to unravel this problem, to tease the threads apart and look at the different aspects that make us feel and act the way we do. If we can understand them we can actually do something about it.

Why me?

Who knows? Why is anyone the way they are? The answer is very complex. It must be a combination of circumstances. Some people are naturally optimistic, some naturally pessimistic. Some have one kind of upbringing, some another.

Some have pleasant experiences in life, some have less pleasant. We learn all the time. By that I mean that our bodies learn. They learn to react in a particular way physically, to produce certain sensations in some situations – and we learn to fear these situations. We shall consider these things further in a later chapter.

One thing is certain. There is no point at all in mulling over the past in an effort to sort out our problems. We must start to deal with our lack of confidence here and now. What is past is past. Forget about it. Going over it again and again could be positvely harmful. We must think only about the future.

Consider another thing. An abundance of confidence, or a lack of confidence, has nothing to do with our ability or with our worth as individuals. It is something which is tacked on to our personality. You can be a pleasant confident person or a pleasant underconfident person. You can be nice or nasty, able or less able whether confident or not. We can take confidence by itself and deal with it, and that is what we are going to do.

Teasing out the strands

We are trying to simplify the problems of the underconfident person, and yet it seems that things are beginning to appear to be rather more complicated than at first. We have the *physical* side of underconfidence. Then we have the mental appreciation of the problem, the cognitive element. We know that we lack confidence. We are aware of it, often very aware. How will we cope with work and social situations? And what about the effects of that condition in the long term. Peter, for example, worried about his underconfidence and the effect it had on his social life and possibly his future career.

All these things have to be dealt with. And more than that. We all have a right to be happy and contented, but that is more difficult if we are lacking in confidence. It's not just not being

12

able to do things. It's not being able to enjoy doing things and all the heartache involved in that situation. We all want to be happy and to enjoy our lives. When we lack confidence the happiness factor is somehow removed from our lives and everything can become dreary.

So how are we to beat this problem? Well, we must start as we have done, by dividing the problem up into its parts. You simply cannot deal with a huge undefined, armorphous problem even if it does exist under the one name: under-confidence. So we have to look for a way into that problem. We have to tackle it at its weakest link. We have to be self-critical and able to analyse our personal difficulties. We have to be strictly honest about it. And we have to set reasonable goals.

Could I suggest some useful tools? You can do a lot with a pencil and paper. Setting things down on paper can be a great advantage. Somehow a problem analysed on paper seems more manageable. You can take it out and look at it. You can strike out or add bits in. You can do your homework and you can get things into perspective. Here are some headings which might help you:

Physical symptoms. What are they? Where do I experience them?
What situations give me the *most* trouble? Why?
What sort of people make me feel that I lack confidence? Why?
What situation would I most like to master?
What situations am I particularly *good* at?

Now we are beginning to make some progress. If you have begun to think about your problem instead of simply accepting it, then you have made a start. But there is a lot to learn yet. Not only do you have to learn what has to be done, but you have to learn to trust your decisions, to trust yourself in any situation. Understanding and trust make for confidence.

So how do you feel about your lack of confidence now? Is there a possibility that you might just be able to do something about it? Is there a way forward? Do you even now feel a little more optimistic than you did? I certainly hope so, because there *is* a way forward and there is every chance that you can come to terms with your problem and really do something about it. But it depends on you. It takes work and effort, but then so does everything else worthwhile in this life. The most important thing is to make a start and to proceed by small steps.

Start now by writing a few notes about your particular situation and then we can proceed.

3
Self-analysis

What are we really like?

Self-analysis can be an absorbing hobby. It can also be very instructive and helpful if you don't overdo it. Understanding yourself is a necessary first step to improving yourself.

You have begun the process. You have had a good look at yourself, thought about yourself. Perhaps you have made a few notes. What have you found out on this voyage of discovery? You must be very honest. We can all fool others but we must *not* fool ourselves. This is not the time for self-deception.

Most of us do have a very accurate idea of what we are like. There is evidence that we do. For example, think of the people we marry. It is surprising how many of us eventually marry an entirely appropriate spouse. Men don't marry their dream woman. They know what they are really like and they marry the right person, almost instinctively. What we are trying to achieve now is a true understanding of what we are really like.

What about those notes we made? Here we put down some thoughts about our particular problem, the things which bother us. We thought about the fact that in some situations we get unpleasant sensations. As a doctor I would call them symptoms. Of course, not everyone will experience these, but certainly everyone who considers himself or herself to be lacking in confidence will have these sensations in some difficult situation.

Symptoms

Imagine that you are at a meeting. Perhaps you don't like meetings, and you are concerned that you might be asked to give a report. This would not be a problem for most people, but you don't feel confident in this particular situation. So you might feel quite ill, and lacking in confidence. You might experience some or all these symptoms: tremor, diarrhoea, sweating, dizziness, palpitations, muscle tension or feelings of panic.

Why do you get these symptoms? Its very simple. Your body has learned to produce them in response to stress, and for you just being in this situation is stressful. The mechanism by which they are produced is well known by doctors, and is related to the production of a substance called adrenaline which stimulates parts of the nervous system. Tackling these symptoms will be part of your treatment and we will talk about that later. Needless to say the presence of these powerful and distressing symptoms is very damaging to your self-confidence.

Situations

A lack of confidence is selective. We can be generally lacking in confidence, of course, but it is almost always worse in some situations, which will be particularly difficult for us. It may be that we have previously had unpleasant experiences in such a situation, or that we have found our symptoms worse. But the reasons don't matter. We are stuck with the result.

Often the situation will be a small gathering or an enclosed space, somewhere we can't get out of easily, or where we are in contact with people we find threatening. Or perhaps it will be where we will have to deal with members of the opposite sex. Where exactly doesn't matter just now. It is enough to note that the phenomenon exists. We shall deal with it later.

People

Much of our lack of confidence is to do with our relations with

16

other people. We can find all sorts of relationships difficult. We might have trouble with a particular boss, or a girlfrield or boyfriend; it might be a waiter or a hairdresser or a car park attendant. Some of these relationships are important and some are not. But all difficult relationships can damage our confidence, and in a way the less important they are the more inadequate we may feel if we can't handle them. We will come back to these problems.

What situation do you most want to master?

What would we like, not just to be able to do, but to be able to do well and to enjoy doing? If you have made a note of this, then this is your goal. If there is a situation you don't like or you avoid, then mastering that is your goal. Make a note of it and keep it at the back of your mind.

What are you good at?

We are all good at something. This is no time for false modesty, everyone has a talent, no matter how small. Many shy underconfident people have great talent, and that talent may be masked by their lack of confidence. It is particularly important that they learn to master their lack of confidence and fulfil their potential. And exploiting that talent gives them a starting point. It allows them to start from strength. If you have a particular ability mark it down as a plus.

What about your image?

What do we mean by image? Is it important? By image I don't mean anything slight or trivial, the sort of image an advertising man might dream up for a product, but the impression of ourselves we give to the world. It is the image of us that others see. It is the person they see. Now that person may not really be us, but it is the part of us that we project and that others see, and it is what they *think* we are like. It has to be genuine and honest. And it is very important.

It is important because we know that if we appear relaxed and competent, people will take us for that and we can afford to feel confident. We can relax in the knowledge that we don't have to try to impress. We will impress just be being what we are.

Sometimes our image is wrong, and doesn't reflect what we are really like. Something gets in the way and obscures our true selves. We are uncomfortable and it shows. We don't do ourselves justice.

By now we know a bit more about ourselves than we did. We know what we are like, or what we would like to be like. But there is that bit in between, something that prevents us from projecting our true image. Is there anything we can do about that?

The trouble is we may not be like that at all. We may not even want to project that image and be thought of in that way. But an observer can only see the image and has no way of seeing the real you. It can be very hard to penetrate that image.

So let us go to self-examination for a moment, to looking at ourselves, at our image. How can we do that? Well, how does anyone look at their image? They use a mirror.

I am perfectly serious. In our quest for self-knowledge we have so far used a pencil and paper. Now we are to use a mirror. We want to see what we really look like, what image we project, how others see us.

Stand in front of a mirror. What impression of yourself do you have? Do you look relaxed? Do you look comfortable? Is your facial expression easy and relaxed, or tense and lined? If it is, what effect does consciously relaxing it have? You may feel silly, but never mind. Try to relax your face. Now let your shoulders come down. Loosen up. Try to move. Walk a few paces. What do you look like? Comfortable or stiff? Relax. Try to walk in a relaxed way.

Now, if you are quite sure that no one is listening, try talking to yourself. No, you're not going mad, you're just doing a simple exercise. Do you look relaxed while you are talking, or do you nod your head or grimace? Practise cultivating a relaxed expression. Practise walking, moving and talking in a relaxed, easy way.

Now, how do you dress? Obviously you consider the way you dress to be perfectly satisfactory, but how would someone else see it? You have an image of the confident person you would like to be. Does your style of dress fit in with that image?

We use dress to project an image. Our dress says something about us. So does our hairstyle. Everything about us relays a message. Are we transmitting the *right* message?

Do you stand with your head down, almost apologising for yourself? Are your shoulders hunched? Do you avoid looking into someone's eyes? We are still dissecting, still teasing out the threads. What we find may be revealing, maybe even be a little painful, because we might not like what we see. I hope that with our new searching eyes we may see some area which could be improved. Remember, we are looking for small improvements, for chinks in the armour of this dreadful underconfidence. So anything we can improve is worth looking for.

I am not suggesting for a moment that you should completely rearrange your appearance. That might be disastrous. After all, we dress to suit our temperament, or the way we feel, and at the moment we don't feel all that different about ourselves. So a sudden change would be out of character. But take note of the things that might be worth changing in the future – posture, manner of walking, dress or make-up if you are a woman.

Perhaps you could consider a small indulgence. You *have*

changed. The act of obtaining this book has meant that you want to change. The self-study you have indulged in so far has changed you, even if it is only a little. It is said that observing something changes it, and you have been critically observing yourself. You are already a more confident person. So what are you going to do about it?

You should change something about your appearance. Not too much, one thing only. Nothing as extreme as a new hairstyle. Perhaps a new item of clothing, or your make-up? Throw away the beret or the flat shoes for a day or two. You might want to take some advice from a workmate, friend or spouse if you have one. How would they like to see you change your appearance? But most of all, what would you – the new, more confident you – like to change?

Go back to your mirror. Stand up straight and look at yourself. Do you like what you see? Is it worth the effort? Is your appearance more appropriate for the person you want to be? I think you have started to change, and change has a momentum of its own. Once started it gets faster. We have made one small insignificant change. But it is a start.

4

Relaxation

Most of us would like to appear relaxed and at ease. If others *think* we are relaxed and comfortable it is much easier for us to *feel* that way. It's a vicious circle. If we are tense we look tense and we make other people ill at ease. That makes us more tense and the situation gets worse. We have to break that spiral. That isn't easy to do, but it is possible if you go about it the right way.

There is another thing we have to take into consideration. We were talking about the unpleasant sensations we get in some situations. These sensations, or symptoms, are due to the fact that we are tense. When we are tense we are stressed. Our bodies put out too much adrenaline so we feel bad. Many of these symptoms are caused by muscle tension, in our neck, or in our limbs. Or it may be in the muscles of our chest wall, making us feel that we can't get enough air. We *need* to relax. It is a fact that we cannot be comfortable, at ease, symptom-free and mentally relaxed if we are *physically* tense. So if we relax physically we will be relaxed mentally.

Why are we tense?

This is a complex subject. In simple terms, we have just learned to be tense, not consciously, but subconsciously. Our bodies have learned to be tense without us knowing. It may have taken years. We have learned to be uncomfortable in certain situations. Our bodies have learned to produce adrenaline in excess and we are not aware of it until we start to get these symptoms. Then we are stuck with it. We are in a downward spiral. The more adrenaline we produce the more

21

tense we feel, and the more tense we feel the more adrenaline we produce.

Panic attacks and overbreathing

If we produce too much adrenaline we can get panic attacks, and there is nothing more undermining to the confidence than a panic attack. In one of these attacks we feel our heart racing and we sweat. We really feel very unwell for a few seconds. Then it passes off. It is unpleasant, but it can do you no harm, apart from undermining your confidence that is. The same applies to any of these unpleasant sensations. None of them can do you any physical damage.

There is one other mechanism that can cause unpleasant sensations. That is the phenomenon of overbreathing. Sometimes we overbreathe without knowing it. This produces spasm in muscles and that can be unpleasant. It can also produce other sensations such as the ones I have mentioned previously. All of these sensations, no matter how they are caused, can occur in stressful situations. You may not be aware of them, but if you stop and take note of what your body is saying to you you will become aware of just why you are feeling uncomfortable. There is almost certainly a very good physical reason for it.

Don't be alarmed by this. If we know what is going on in our bodies we know that we can do something about it. Knowing that we have a physical cause for the way we feel gives us a way of tackling the problem. It gives us a chink in the armour of our underconfidence, a way in.

What can we do about it?

We have to *learn* to relax. It's as simple as that. Simple, but not easy. It takes hard work, but it *is* possible. First we have to learn how to control our breathing. Both relaxation and breathing control are achieved by learning special exercises.

We have to make time to practise and it takes weeks of effort to learn properly. But it is worth the effort as we are learning techniques we will be able to use the rest of our lives.

The relaxation exercises I am going to describe aren't the only ones, of course. Some yoga exercises may be just as good, and antenatal relaxation exercises are excellent. But you *have* to learn some form of relaxation, and the relaxation and breathing exercises below are as good as any. They have been used successfully by many people.

Relaxation exercises

You need a bit of peace and quiet if you are going to learn to relax. You should find a warm quiet room with a comfortable chair or perhaps a bed. Allow about twenty minutes and practise every day. It isn't as easy as it sounds. There are always other things to do, other distractions. But this is important, so try to find the time.

Sit down in your chair and make yourself comfortable. You cannot relax if you are cold, so make sure the room is warm enough for you. Also ensure that your arms, back and head are well supported. Breathe slowly and evenly. Try to be calm.

Now you can start your exercises. You have to unlock those tense muscles. Begin with your right hand. Squeeze your fist tight. Hold that tightness for a moment. Don't overdo it. Now relax your fist. Do it suddenly and quickly. Feel the relaxation coming into your hand, feel it flowing up your arm. Enjoy the sensation of relaxation in your entire arm up to the shoulder. Pause for a moment and breathe slowly.

Do exactly the same thing with the left arm. Squeeze and relax. Enjoy that feeling of relaxation in your arm, enjoy the warmth. Now slow your breathing. Breathe slowly and evenly.

Turn your attention to your shoulders. If you have a

tendency to be tense then you will feel that tension in your shoulders. They may even be painful. Lift your shoulders up and hold them there. Again feel the tightness coming into your shoulders and neck. Hold it for a moment. Now relax suddenly, letting the feeling of relaxation flood into your shoulders. Breathe slowly and evenly again for a moment or two.

Next, push your neck back so that you begin to feel your neck muscles getting tight. Again it is your neck which is often the seat of most tension so tensing it may be uncomfortable. Tighten those muscles and hold it for a moment. Now relax suddenly. Feel the relaxation flooding into your neck and shoulders. Breathe slowly.

Now tighten up your facial muscles. Clench your teeth and furrow your brow. Hold that tightness. Now relax. Enjoy the relaxation. Relax your neck, shoulders and arms and breathe slowly.

Move on down your body now. Tighten up your abdominal muscles. Pull your stomach in. Make yourself as thin as you can. Hold that. Now relax the muscles as before. Feel the relaxation and breathe slowly.

Next, tighten up your leg muscles. Do that by pushing your toes into the floor. Feel the tightness coming into your feet, calves and thighs. Hold that tension for just a moment, being careful not to produce a cramp in your calf muscles. Relax the muscles and notice the relaxation feeling flow into your entire leg. You have now relaxed your whole body.

Turn your attention now to your breathing. Really work at that. Slow your breathing down. You should be able to slow your breathing to about six breaths a minute. Concentrate on slow, even breathing. This really helps relaxation. Continue this slow breathing and try to hold on to the feeling of relaxation.

Now think calm, warm thoughts. Think of something pleasant, something relaxing. A holiday beach might be suitable, but you can think of anything you like. Wallow in the relaxation. One word of warning. Relaxation isn't easy to achieve so don't expect too much. It may take many sessions before you can really relax, particularly if you are habitually tense. When you do achieve relaxation you will know. It is a very pleasant sensation for a tense person. It is a feeling of warmth right down to your finger tips, a feeling of floating, of calmness. When you have relaxed yourself and slowed your breathing and you want to finish the session, count down 'three, two, one, *finish*'. Now you are back in the real world.

If you have difficulty learning to relax, record the exercises on a tape recorder at the same speed as you might like to do them in practice. Now relax to the sound of your own voice, taking about twenty minutes to do all the exercises.

Breathing exercises

Some people habitually overbreathe. This blows carbon dioxide out of the lungs and thus produces a state of tetany, or muscle spasm. In other words, breathing too hard makes your muscles tense. You have to learn to control your breathing just as you have to learn to relax your muscles.

How can you do that? Normally when you are at rest you don't use your chest muscles for breathing at all. That may sound odd but it is true. When you are sitting watching television your chest muscles should be more or less at rest. You use your stomach muscles and your diaphragm for breathing. If you are using your chest muscles, or if you are taking frequent deep breaths or sighs, then you are doing it wrongly. This is a matter of habit, something you have developed by long practice, without even knowing that you are doing it. Now you have to put it right.

You can correct your breathing by practising doing it the right way. The best time to do that is when you are watching television. Place one hand on your chest, the other on your stomach. The hand on your stomach should be moving, the one on your chest should be still. If the hand on your chest is moving you should concentrate on relaxing your chest muscles and allowing your stomach muscles to do the work. Just stay in this position for a while and try to correct your breathing. Do it as often and for as long as you need to, but don't overdo it. Your breathing will take care of itself if you give it time.

How to use your skills

It is one thing to be able to relax and to breathe properly in the privacy of your own home. It is another to be able to do this outside to your advantage. Learning this takes time and effort. You want to be able to relax at meetings, at parties or on the train or bus. You want to be able to feel comfortable wherever you are and to project the image of relaxed confidence. That is what this book is all about.

You have to start somewhere, so start at home. Begin in your bedroom, then do it in front of the television. Now try it at work or on the bus – anywhere. One of the advantages of learning to relax is that it lets you spot early on when you are getting tense, and this allows you to start relaxing earlier than you otherwise might. That doesn't mean going through all those tightening and loosening exercises. Those are just to give you a start. You should be able to relax now by just sitting comfortably and breathing slowly. You should have learnt enough about your body to be able to take some control of it. Just slow your breathing and relax and, if you have done your homework, that should be enough.

Your new image

What is the image you project now? Can you sit at a meeting or at a party and look calm and relaxed? What do your clothes say about you? Can you walk and move in a relaxed way? And what will others think about you? Most of all, what do *you* feel like? Perhaps you feel a little bit more comfortable. Perhaps you are just a little bit more confident than you were. We have made a start; now let us move on.

5

Facing the World Outside

We have been talking about techniques that you can practise at home, or exercises that will strengthen our confidence, but we have not talked much about things that we can actually do out in the community. There is a reason for that. It might be possible to give you a list of responses to different situations, or tell you things that you might say to people on different occasions. That would be easy, but it is not the way forward for you.

Confidence comes from *within* ourselves. We have to build confidence from basic principles. There can be no short cuts. Any small advantage gained from an attempt to cut corners would be shortlived. So let us continue with the hard slog, knowing that there is the only one way forward. What comes now might be a little painful. Some things have to be faced and now is a good time to get them out of the way.

Self-criticism

So far we have been looking at ourselves very critically, reorganizing ourselves. We have made a few changes. Now we might have to make a few more. What we have to do now is to look at ourselves again, this time not as we see ourselves, but as others might see us. Why would that be painful?

We might not like what we see, or we might not particularly enjoy this sort of dissection of our character. What we are going to do now is to look not so much at our character as at our behaviour – at the way we act and at the things we do, more precisely, the things we do wrongly.

Do you put people off?

If you are lacking in confidence it might be because of a difficulty communicating with other people. And that might be because you not only project an image unfavourable to yourself, you may actually put people off by your behaviour.

There is no point in going over the past, but some consideration of past events is inevitable. We will do as little of it as possible, as it can be distressing. We all have such events in our past. Often they are very trivial, but we remember them because of the embarrassment they caused. We are now going to look at them in the hope that we can learn from them.

How do we behave?

We must consider how we behave in certain situations, or perhaps how we behave every time we meet the same situation. Do we do it wrongly? This is different from the exercises we have been doing up to now where we have been considering the detail of the way we dress or sit or walk. Now we are thinking about the way we act, not so much about the way we talk as about the things we say. How does this appear to others?

Remember a past encounter

You may well remember some event or encounter which was less than satisfactory from your point of view. You may well know exactly why it went wrong. Knowing that is not the same as doing something about it. But you may well not realize what is unsatisfactory about your relationships. We all have the ability for self-discovery just as we all have the capacity of self-delusion. Now is the time for realism.

Do you put people off? And if so why? Let us consider some possibilities, then you can make up your own mind. Later on we can work out ways of dealing with our difficulties. For the moment think of a particular relationship or encounter which

29

was less than successful. Perhaps you have always wondered just why it didn't work the way you would have liked.

What goes wrong?

Only you can answer such a question. But there are some things that might have gone wrong, and they might still be going wrong and spoiling your relationships now. If your relationships with other people are in some way unsatisfactory you can never have the confidence to know that they will go better in the future. You actually have to do something about it.

As always, the first thing to do is to look at the problem. Try not to look with your own eyes, rather with the eyes of the other person involved in the encounter. What did he, or she, see? What didn't he or she like about the event, or think you did wrong?

The answer is almost certainly straightforward. There may, of course, be an explanation that has nothing to do with you. There are many reasons why things go wrong, but you should choose some event which you think went wrong because of something you may have done, or the way you may have acted. Why did it go wrong?

Perhaps you were too enthusiastic, or tried too hard, or smothered the person with enthusiasm or even with affection. You may have offered or done too much. People 'back off' if you intrude on their privacy, or remove their initiative. People don't want to be in someone's debt unless they choose to be.

This happened to a girl I know. A boy at her work asked her to do some shopping for him because he was going to have to work late. She liked the boy and was flattered to have been asked. I think the boy liked her too and had an ulterior motive for asking her to help. But the girl not only did the shopping he asked for, she bought other things which she thought he might like, including some flowers that she thought might brighten up his apartment. Instead of being grateful to the girl, the boy was embarrassed and as a result seemed unkind. What might have been a very satisfactory relationship just didn't get started. It would have been better if the girl had just done the shopping she had been asked to do.

So you may do too much, or seem overanxious to please. Or there is the other extreme. You may be embarrassed by the attention of others and so seem to be diffident and un-interested. You may well be extremely cautious in your dealings with others, or too much on your guard, too frightened of hazarding yourself, too scared of getting hurt or taken advantage of. We are all a bit like that. We have to be because it is a dangerous world. But it is a matter of degree. Are you too cautious?

Be yourself

Or are you 'dishonest' about yourself in other ways? Do you pretend to be someone you are not? Perhaps you aren't aware of doing that, but it might be true just the same. We all act a part, but some people do that more than others and sometimes it shows. Do you pretend to be the great outdoor type when you are really more fond of your own fireside? Do you make casual remarks which suggest great achievements in the past? You may not deliberately make up facts about your past, but you may try to give a certain impression just the same. That can work to your advantage for a while, but in the long run you can't pretend. Your true personality will come out and then you are in trouble. It is better to just be yourself.

Can people talk to you?

Is it just that you are absolutely impossible to talk to? It may be that you don't listen to the answers people give to your questions. Or you may not answer the questions people ask

31

you because you are too intent on thinking up your next question. You may simply have lost the art of conversation because you are lacking in confidence and are too keen to please. You may not concentrate during a conversation. That may be because you are self-conscious, but how is the person you are talking to to know that? He or she can only know what he or she sees and hears.

We have already talked about the business of being relaxed and appearing relaxed. We should be on the way to mastering those particular arts by now. Remember that someone who says little and stays calm and quiet is always taken to be wise. But one can't stay quiet forever. Let us now think about conversation and relationships.

The art of conversation

Surely a conversation is a simple natural event? Yes, for many people it is just that. But for the shy or self-conscious it can be a trial, loaded with difficulties. We may even have to learn the art of conversation. That isn't difficult and with practice it will become natural and easy. Try talking to yourself, in the car, or at home. Talk to people on the train or on the bus.

There are some things you have to remember. One is to concentrate, actually listen to what is being said. Think about your responses, try to say something intelligent and don't speak just for the sake of speaking. That means that you will have to allow silences to occur in the conversation, which can be difficult. But remember that you have new powers. You now have the ability to relax. You are more at ease so silences become tolerable.

Don't force the conversation just for the sake of doing so. Let it take its own course. Don't say silly things just for the sake of appearing clever. Listen to what is said. Learn to identify humour and sarcasm, so that you don't take everything too seriously. Let people talk to you – don't talk *at* people.

Eye-to-eye contact can be a problem. You don't know just how much you should look at the person to whom you are talking. Meet his or her eyes too much and you might appear arrogant, too little and you appear disinterested. You have to strike a balance, and that comes with practice. The more confidence you get, the more conversations you have, the less of a problem these things become. Don't worry about them. Just notice that they are there. You can try to sort them out, but in the long run they will sort themselves out.

Practise finishing a conversation. Learn a few gambits to use when you feel that a conversation has reached a natural conclusion. You could say, 'Well, I have to go now,' or 'It's been nice meeting you,' or anything you like. But learn how to stop a conversation. Some people find that very difficult, but really it's just a matter of rehearsal and practice, of learning how to manage a conversation. When you can control your body, or a relationship, or a conversation, then you can begin to have confidence in your performance. Confidence builds on confidence.

More work

So there is some more work to do. You have to take note of the way you behave in public. But you should also watch the way other people do things. Choose someone who does it well. See how he conducts encounters, look in detail at the things he says and the way he says them. Of course you can't just copy someone else. That doesn't work. But it will give you ideas about the way you can change your approach. Try to make small changes first. Perhaps try to talk a little less, or listen a little more. Make whatever small improvements you can. Remember, we are in the business of making small advances, knowing that overall our performance will improve, and with it our confidence.

Look right, talk right, feel right. Learn all the time. These are things you can practise yourself. But confidence is about relationships with others. What is their part in all this? How do other people manage us? That is what we shall look at next.

6

Interacting with Others

Confidence is mostly about our relationships with other people. It takes two people to have a conversation or a relationship of any sort. What do other people contribute to that relationship? Thinking about that will be a change from the constant consideration of our own difficulties. It's time we had a break.

Most people in this world are kind and considerate, and some are perceptive and thoughtful. But there are also people who deliberately exploit others knowingly. Others do it as a matter of habit, and they have no idea how much unhappiness they can cause. We have all met them, maybe at work or in some other situation. They take advantage of their position if they can.

Surprisingly, these individuals can be very pleasant in themselves. They seem to have a lack of awareness in their relationships. People who are actually cruel are fairly uncommon. There is very little we can do about them. We should just abandon them to their fate.

Other people's attitudes

Watching other people tackle the problems of life can be entertaining as well as instructive. Many individuals are abusive or unpleasant because they have difficulties in their own relationships. They are also refugees from the real world. I have observed them over many years.

Because I am a doctor, the people I have worked with most and observed most tend to be doctors and patients. I'm sure doctors aren't very different from people in any other walk of life. They have the same problems, even though they are often

35

expected to be immune from some of the difficulties other people meet.

One thing a doctor is meant to have is confidence. No patient wants to go and see a doctor who doesn't seem to be confident, because it may seem that he doesn't know what he is doing even though he really is competent. Doctors aren't taught how to present themselves to the public. They have to learn this themselves, and some of them don't do it very well.

We all know about the hospital consultant who treats his patients with rudeness and incivility. Some hospital doctors work in hospitals to escape from the real world. A hospital is a very protected environment. Doctors are surrounded by all the trappings of the hospital, the sterile instruments, the nurses in their uniforms. Their arrogance is a cover for their insecurity. It's just a pity that the poor patients have to suffer.

Personal interactions

Hospital life can provide other examples of interactions between people. My first encounter with it was as a medical student – here one is bottom of every ladder and the butt of everyone's sarcasm and humour. Much of the teaching is at the bedside and is done by those same consultants who can be so rude to patients. You can imagine what they can do to students.

Most consultants, of course, are very reasonable. But I'm talking now about the ones whose ward rounds we used to dread. They would think it clever to terrorize students, and they had a knack of picking out the least confident and making an example of him. They used their position to their own advantage, to boost their own ego, and it was unforgiveable.

It took me a few years to sort this out in my own mind, and I can still remember the day truth dawned. I was working in a teaching hospital, and one of my duties was to go on the teaching ward round with the consultant. He used to terrorize me as well as the students by asking all sorts of awkward questions. I never seemed to know the answer and that looked very bad in front of the students.

One day I couldn't answer a question so I turned the tables and asked the consultant for the answer. He huffed and puffed but I insisted, in front of the students, that he told us what the answer was because I thought it was important. It became clear that he didn't know the answer himself. He was bluffing.

The next day I asked him another question and he didn't know the answer again. He stopped annoying me after that, and for a while stopped taking the students at all. I found myself doing all the teaching on the ward. That was an interesting experience.

I found that the students knew much more than I thought. If they were given time and encouragement they could work out the answers to questions, and they would make a stab at anything they were asked. I developed a friendly relaxed style. Thinking about it, that was done for my benefit as much as for the students. The consultant could only teach in an atmosphere of tension and confrontation that masked his own insecurity. I couldn't manage that situation. I could only teach if I and everyone else was relaxed.

That is not to say that I was confident in that situation. I certainly wasn't. But I managed my lack of confidence differently. I produced a sympathetic atmosphere so that any shortcomings I might display would be understood and allowed for by the students. That helped most of the students as well, but it left a problem in reverse. One or two of the students exploited the situation to display their own know-ledge and their supposed superiority. There were some students I simply dreaded having on my ward round.

I had to solve that problem too, so I simply asked them questions to which they couldn't possibly know the answers, and allowed a long silence to occur as we all waited for the answer. They soon learned to stand at the back of the group of students and to keep quiet. The rest of us could then get on with the ward round.

Games people play

What I had been doing was learning about the games people play with each other. Many people are very competitive. They play games all the time, and they play to win. Those of us who are less confident don't play those games. We aren't particularly interested in scoring points off others. That isn't to say that we aren't ambitious or able. It is a matter of temperament and inclination. But unfortunately these games can be important.

To take my example of the teaching hospital, these same students have to sit examinations which are often oral. They have to sit opposite a professor or senior doctor and answer questions. Some of these eminent men can draw answers out of students and put them at ease, but some are just plain ignorant. I have met both types, and I have examined students myself. It is easy to spot the less confident student and give him time to settle. It's surprising the results that can be obtained.

These same situations exist in industry and even in social encounters. We have all met people who want to dominate us. There are all sorts of psychological reasons for the way people behave, but the result is the same. Unless we are aware of what is going on, we can be the losers.

What about social situations? I can remember meeting an old friend in the city one day. I hadn't seen him for years so I was very pleased to meet him. He shook my hand warmly and we exchanged greetings. Then he said, 'What's the matter. You're not looking at all well.' We had lunch together, but all the time I was thinking, 'Why don't I look well? What's wrong with me.'

I soon forgot about the incident, but a year later I met him again. 'How are you?' he asked. 'You're not looking at all well.' Then I remembered what had happened the previous year, and I had my answer. 'That's funny,' I said, 'I feel absolutely great. But you're not looking too well yourself.'

My friend worked in business. He was a sales representative and he lived to some extent on his wits. He was a naturally competitive individual and had developed ploys to keep himself on top of any situation. When he met me he naturally wanted to assert himself and his way of doing that was to suggest that there was something wrong with me. It put me off balance for a moment, diverted my attention. If I had been a business rival it would have given him an advantage. The trouble was that he had developed the habit of scoring points off other people in the business situation and now did it automatically.

I didn't mind that so long as I knew what was going on. I didn't want to play that sort of game, but if I knew about it I didn't mind. We are still the best of friends.

Do we need to play games?

I don't think it would be wise to try to compete with the games players. Let's leave that to the experts. We have agreed that there are no tricks and no short cuts. We don't need them anyway. But how do we deal with a games player?

The best way is to do exactly what we have been trying to achieve right from the beginning. Project an air of quiet confidence, even if you don't feel it. Don't be flustered by anyone, certainly not by someone who needs to play games to keep *his* confidence. Just relax and watch. You don't have to join in.

But it does no harm to let the person who is playing games know that you know what he is doing. A remark or a smile can do that. That is enough to assert your superiority.

Now we have to learn how to improve our performance in public. That is what we will do next.

7

Improving Our Social Skills

Preparation

What can we do to make our lives more comfortable, those difficult situations easier to manage?

We have already learnt about relaxation and how to project a confident image. Is there anything else we can do? If we know that we are going to have to attend an event that we will find difficult, is there any way we can prepare for it? Is there any way we can use those hours of discomfort which preceed a social event or a business meeting, or perhaps a speech?

I don't think we need to just accept that things may be difficult. We can prepare by practising our relaxation exercises as often as we can. But there are also ways that we can develop our relaxing to help us further. If we are to do that we have to use our imagination.

We all have some imagination. Sometimes it is too vivid and we imagine all sorts of difficulties. That is counterproductive. But a normal sensible imagination can be used to our advantage. We can rehearse and practise any situation we find difficult in our imagination.

No actor would consider appearing on the stage without sufficient rehearsal, because he knows that he would make a fool of himself. The pressure of performing in front of an audience would make him perform unnaturally. He might forget his lines. He might 'die' as actors call it. So an actor will always rehearse and practise before any new part.

If you find some ordinary events just as stressful as an actor might find performing in a new play you might consider preparing for that party or business meeting in advance, privately.

If you are already doing relaxation exercises, you will remember that when you finished doing them you had a period of quiet and relaxation? That is the time to use your imagination. Imagine the situation you are going to have to face, picture it in detail. Think of your arrival, who might be there when you go in, what they might say to you, what you might reply. Go through the whole evening in your imagination if you can.

As we have already found out, you might experience any unpleasant sensations that you normally get in the real situation. Use your breathing and relaxation techniques to deal with those symptoms. That is good practice too. But do some planning as well. Decide how you arc going to handlc the different encounters.

It may be that the actual event is nothing like what you imagine, so be prepared to adapt if necessary. You can't afford to be too rigid. But the exercise is useful and interesting just the same, and worth doing.

Keeping records

A friend of mine joined the Royal Navy. He was a very ambitious and competitive person and he was determined to do well. He was certainly not lacking in confidence. He realised early on that making a good impression on one's superiors was important, so he devised a system for doing just that.

He knew that remembering people's names and personal particulars was important. It is very flattering if someone remembers you and your particular interests. But how do you do that if you have a terrible memory and never have the least idea who you are talking to, even though you have only met them recently? It's a problem many of us have.

My friend worked out a solution. He started a 'Kardex' of everyone he met. After a party or a meeting he went home and wrote down the names of everyone he had met and as much as he could remember about them. He soon built up a dossier on a large number of influential people. Then, before going out to a party or meeting, he would look up the guest list, or try to work out who might be there. He could then 'read up' their details and prepare himself for meeting them.

If he had been caught my friend might have been taken for a spy. Keeping records like that isn't the sort of thing that I would be comfortable doing, particularly if it was being done for purely social reasons. But it might have a place in certain situations.

Business representatives keep similar notes about clients. A sales representative can't afford to forget the name or personal details of a client, so before he makes a call he may well get out a card with the client's details on it so that he can refresh his memory. I think that is a quite legitimate exercise. If you have difficulty organizing yourself, good notes might be worth having.

Some doctors in private practice do the same thing. Good medical records are essential, so a doctor will commit a lot of information to paper after a consultation. Some of them may then turn over the sheet of paper and write a few further notes on the back, such as 'Just moved to new house,', or 'Son just starting school.' These little *aide memoires* are useful. At the next consultation with the patient the doctor can say, 'And how is your son getting on at his new school?' The patient or the client will be flattered and impressed.

Do you think these little ploys are cheating? I'm not very keen on them myself, but there are situations where they can be useful, particularly in business where you have to make an impression. If you are lacking in confidence it is easy to get flustered and to forget people's names and who they are. It might be well worth while doing a little homework to get things sorted out in your mind.

Meeting people

I have another problem. I can often remember a face, but never a name. I can shake hands with someone and instantly forget their name. I'm not the only one with this problem. It happens because one is just a little flustered. You tend to rush things and to forget what's important. Again there is a ploy which can help. Just watch how many people use it when they are introduced to you.

When you are introduced shake hands, but repeat the name of the person to whom you are being introduced. Don't just say 'Hello', say, 'I'm pleased to meet you *Mr Brown*.' That way you imprint the name in your mind. You might even repeat it to yourself later on so that you will learn it and remember it.

If you really have terrible problems remembering details about people the best thing to do is to brazen it out. Just say quite candidly that you are sorry but you can't remember names. Most people will understand. Don't be too apologetic about it, it's a common failing. Just be matter of fact about it.

Take your time

Really skilful people often seem to have plenty of time. Sportsmen and musicians, for example, rarely seem to be rushed. They have the confidence to make time. It's a skill you have to develop. If you are introduced to someone and you can't quite remember what you should know about them, don't rush it. Be prepared to make small talk for a while. You will remember what you thought you had forgotten. Or if you don't, the person to whom you are talking may say something that reminds you. If that doesn't happen, you always have the time to say, 'I'm sorry, I know I should know you, but I can't remember where we met.' That doesn't give offence.

It is better to be quiet, to look relaxed and at ease, and let things take their course. If you have the beginnings of that inner confidence, then these things become more and more easy.

Social skills training

This is a term used by psychologists to explain the sort of things we have been talking about. People who lack confidence have to learn 'social skills'. We all have to learn social skills as we go through life just as we have to learn manners.

We are learning all the time. Some of us have a better facility for learning than others, and some of us just learn wrongly. If that has happened to you, then you have to do something about it.

You have to start learning again, but this time you have to learn the right social skills. That means looking critically at the way you behave in public and thinking of what you can do to improve your performance. I have mentioned some of the things you can do. You will have to work out other ways of improving your performance.

What I am talking about is really changing your attitude to your problems. You cannot go on accepting things as they are. You are developing skills of relaxation and of meeting and dealing with other people. You must build on success. If you are beginning to feel more comfortable in some situations, don't leave it at that. Try to find ways of going forwards.

You must improve your social skills. That covers every aspect of your life. You must always be critical of yourself. Open your eyes to the way the things you do appear to others and think how you can improve them. This is an ongoing process with which you must persist perhaps for the rest of your life.

That isn't as difficult as it sounds. The fact is that you will soon start to do it subconsciously. You will cease to notice that you are doing it. It will quite simply be part of the new, more confident you. Now, shouldn't you be beginning to act more like a confident person? We shall consider that next.

8

Starting to Fulfil Our Expectations

By now it should be clear that there is a path for us to go down. We have already started our journey and we should feel the beginnings of confidence by now. That means that we should be looking for ways to expand our lives, looking for more things to do. We want some reward for our hard work and we deserve it.

Aiming towards a goal

We must have thought of things that we would like to do but have been avoiding. At the beginning of this book I suggested that you should pick out one thing that you really wanted to achieve and to keep that as a goal. I don't know when you will feel confident enough to tackle that particular goal. You certainly shouldn't rush it. There is merit in taking time, and you alone can decide what you want to do and when you want to do it.

First of all, start thinking of things you can do that aren't quite so intimidating. Think of simple things that you might have been avoiding; we often avoid difficult situations without really realizing it. It's time you started practising difficult situations, particularly those you may have been avoiding because they give you so much trouble.

Of course your new confidence may be showing in your work or in your social life, but you should have even bigger returns. You should be starting to fulfil your own expectations of life. So look around and see what you might be doing to expand your experience of, and your enjoyment of life.

Some suggestions

If you are feeling more confident, say, at work, what else can you do to expand your life? If you are a shy, selfconscious person it may be that you have allowed your world to contract. You may have denied yourself some of the pleasures of life which others take for granted. This is not your fault, but the natural result of your lack of confidence.

So where do you start? The world is full of things that other people do, but it may well be that none of them really appeal to you. You can't suddenly manufacture an interest in photography, for example. You have to exploit an honest interest. If you try to create an interest in something you don't really care about you will end up in trouble.

One thing which often works is to start with an interest in some kind of physical activity. Getting fit is always worth while, because not only does it bring you into contact with other people, it has benefits of its own. If you are fit, you feel good. Anything which makes you feel good is worth doing. I learned to swim late in life, something I had always wanted to be able to do. I had always felt out of it on holiday with others, simply because I couldn't swim. So eventually I made up my mind that I would just get on with it and I attended classes at my local swimming baths. I didn't meet too many people or make lifelong friends, but it is one of the best things I ever did and I now swim regularly to keep fit. It gives me confidence in some situations, and I know that I could at least make an effort to save any of my children from drowning if they ever fell into the water. Confidence comes in all shapes and forms. And the sense of achievement I had when I eventually swam a length was tremendous.

Perhaps you can already swim well. But you may not be able to dance. Now there are dance studios and dance classes everywhere, so you might try that. Being fit feels good. And if you can do it with other people so much the better. There are many sports clubs around and you could do worse than join one of them – provided that you have an interest in that particular sport.

Remember always to have reasonable expectations initially. Don't try too hard, or to do too much too soon. Build on your successes. You must do *something*, but it doesn't have to be physical. You might have an interest in photography or in needlework. One thing is sure, if you join a club or society you will be made most welcome. There is nothing a club needs more than new members, and the members of a club will be delighted to see you. It's good to be made welcome and to feel yourself to be amongs friends. An interest in your subject shared with others will be the cornerstone of your relationship.

At the end of the day it is relationships with people that are important. It is usually people who are intimidating, not places or events. We have discussed many ways of making these relationships easier. Let relationships develop. Remember all that has been said. Don't rush things, don't be overanxious, don't smother people. *Just be yourself*.

Holidays

One area where we meet others is on holiday. The annual holiday is one of the great events of the year. We look forward to it with anticipation verging on excitement. What will happen? Whom will we meet? At least that's the way it should be. For some people it may be spoiled by worry. Or again they may expect too much.

Young people's and singles holidays are all the rage nowadays. The holidaymaker is almost guaranteed a good time, and he or she is *expected* to form relationships. Comradeship is all part of the deal. It might be that this would be the ideal holiday for you, but it might also be a disaster if you aren't naturally convivial. You might just be forced into situations you don't really wish to be in.

Choose your holiday carefully, one that will attract people of your own age group and interests. For example, a skiing holiday might be the right sort of thing for you. But don't stake everything on meeting the man or woman of your life. Mind you, that can and does happen on holiday sometimes, so go with an open mind. You never know.

Holiday problems

You may have special difficulties about holidays. Perhaps you aren't too happy about flying, or you may not have anyone to take a holiday with, or you may not like the idea of going abroad and having to deal with foreigners. Difficulties are made to be be overcome. You have to think of ways of getting round them.

If you have trouble with flying, that can be dealt with. Your doctor may be able to arrange for you to see a psychologist who can help you with that sort of phobia, but in any case you have learned techniques for dealing with that yourself. Remember your relaxation exercises and how to practise difficult situations in your mind? If you have booked a holiday abroad and paid for it there is a strong incentive to get on with it. Prepare for it as carefully as you would prepare for any other stressful event.

Dealing with foreigners and the uncertainties of going abroad is another problem. But remember that the anticipation of events is often worse than the event itself. Just decide to go and when you get there it won't be as difficult as you think. If you go with a tour company, you would be surprised just how helpful the company representative can be. He or she will help you with any problems you might have, and will often arrange your social life if that is what you wish. It is very much in their interest that you have a good time.

Finding companions

Finding someone to go on holiday with can certainly be a

problem if you are not married. Singles holidays come in many forms, and can be excellent for an older person, perhaps for a widow. But the world is full of single people who are looking for someone with whom to go on holiday. Finding them is the problem.

For an older person there are now groups such as retirement associations, the main purpose of which is to arrange holidays for their members. That might be as bad as going with an 'under 30' holiday package, but it is worth looking at. Sports clubs at work often arrange skiing holidays and the like, and are keen to find members to share the cost. Or just having the confidence to ask around at work or at a club or society might be the answer. You never know who might be in the same position as yourself.

Other ways of changing your life

You might think of learning to drive. If you lack confidence you might find that a rather daunting prospect, but think of the possible gains, the independence and mobility you would gain. It could open up an entire new world for you, and it could bring you into contact with others. People are always looking for transport for days out or for holidays. We will talk a bit more about how we might go about learning to drive and similar activities later.

There are many ways of expanding your horizons, some of them quite drastic. It pays to be cautious. You might think of changing your job for example, or of leaving school earlier than you intended, or going into full-time education, which can be a good way of meeting the right people and getting on. You might think of other even more drastic measures, such as getting married or even getting a divorce if you are married and unhappy. Be careful here though!

Golden rules

Some of these things may be appropriate for you. But they could go disastrously wrong. Major decisions in this life have to be carefully thought out and considered. Don't rush into any action which might be irreversible.

This is the golden rule. Make any major changes in your life you might be considering *because* you are feeling more confident, not in the hope that you may feel more confident as a result of any change you make. Your new job, or your new marital situation, may be just as difficult as the last one if the cause of some of your problems was your lack of confidence. You must fix that first.

We have talked about how you can do that in practical ways. Start with the small practical changes and then, when you are feeling more confident and more able, think about how you want to expand your life and move on.

That is not to say that changing your job or your education is not possible or desirable. It may be exactly what you are needing, but be careful. Plan your decisions well, taking into account every aspect of the problem. Take advice. As always, give it time. See how the idea seems after a week or two. Work out all the possible consequences. If you still feel that a major change in your life is needed, and that you can cope with the consequences, then go ahead.

Some changes in your life you can arrange yourself. Some happen in spite of your wishes, and they can destroy your confidence. We will consider some of these changes in the next chapter.

9

Why Do We Lose Confidence?

Why have you found yourself in a situation where you are self-conscious and lacking in confidence? So far we have only touched on that subject and I don't think we should dwell on it now. The only reason we are considering it is so that we can learn some lessons and gain some benefit.

Some reasons

The reason why you have lost confidence may be perfectly obvious. It might well be due to one of life's events, such as bereavement or divorce. You may not have thought of this event as a cause of your problem, perhaps because you only became aware of it many months after the event happened.

Many of us just *seem* to be born lacking in confidence, but this state is often aggravated by some misfortune. But why not forget about the cause? Why not just get on with life as has already been suggested? The answer is that we have to take note of the events that happen to us because they simply won't go away. They lurk at the back of our minds, and no matter how much we would like to forget them, they remain there like unexorcised ghosts.

However, we should try to forget about them, get them in proportion, working always for the future. There is no point in going over the details of the event that brought you unhappiness. All that will do is to make you relive that unhappiness, and bring you further pain. But there are some general points which should be made because they may help you.

The first thing is that no matter what has caused you such unhappiness, you are not the only one to have experienced it and others have survived. This is not a callous statement, just the truth. You have to survive and you have to rebuild. You have to work at rebuilding your confidence. That is a positive and necessary thing to do.

Maybe your problems began not with one major event, but a series of seemingly trivial events that combined against you. If you are young and having problems with your confidence, that is what may have happened to you. You may not even have been aware of these events, because you haven't been looking for them.

Psychologists believe in the theory that we learn throughout our lives. I don't mean that we learn consciously. I mean that our bodies learn to respond in certain ways to different situations. That is why we develop certain physical sensations or symptoms in situations where we are *phobic*. These are often social or work situations, although it is possible to be phobic about anything from mice to lifts. Phobias are a subject in themselves and they are dealt with at length in other books (See, for example, *Overcoming Tension*).

Quite simply, if you have a bad experience in a situation, you feel stressed. You produce substances that cause physical effects, and you don't want to be exposed to that sort of physical unpleasantness again. Some people are easily stressed, and some are fortunate enough rarely to feel stressed. It's the luck of the draw.

Stress

If it is in your nature to be easily stressed, things such as embarrassment in a social setting will cause you difficulty. Both you and your body will remember them. Likewise, if you are exposed to one large stressful event, you may have physical problems that might not afflict a less sensitive person.

However, it is just that. If we are sensitive individuals we are more aware of our problems, and the more aware we are the more problems we get. It's not surprising that we find that our confidence is eroded. Even at a young age, in adolescence or younger, we can become aware that we are lacking in confidence. It may be the price we pay for being sensitive, imaginative people.

We can live with our problems up to a point, but it can be unpleasant, particularly in adolescence.

Adolescence

I sometimes wish that I could go back and live my life again with the benefit of the experience I now have. Certainly adolescence would be much easier, because I would have more confidence. We all would. Adolescence is difficult because we are entering the unknown. And that unknown can appear frightening and dangerous to our ego and our confidence.

That is because we are beginning to have to develop relationships with members of the opposite sex. Instead of just going round in groups of our friends, we have to develop single relationships with girls or boys. This is all to do with growing up. Powerful feelings and emotions are part of life, and falling in love, getting married and having children is still the norm. In adolescence we are preparing for these events in later life.

Our self-esteem can be very fragile when we are young. As we get older we get used to rebuffs and learn to take them, but when we are young rejection can be very painful. It happens to us all, and it's always painful.

It's also a vicious circle. If you had the confidence to make the first move there would be no problem. If you had the confidence to be yourself and to relax, your relationships would be more successful. But you have to have the confidence first.

One thing you *can* be confident about is that it will work out all right in the end. Nothing makes for confidence like the passage of time. And those individuals who are so competent in adolescence aren't necessarily the winners in the long run. What matters is the establishment of lasting satisfying relationships, and that is a skill quite different from the ability to have a surfeit of boyfriends or girlfriends.

One thing that might help is the realisation that most people, both girls and boys, are as sensitive and caring as we are ourselves. And they have the same hangups. They should get together and help each other. And of course girls and boys do get together – all that is needed is the courage to get over the initial approach.

If you have real troubles in adolescence, problems more serious than those I have mentioned, you must talk to someone about it. Your parents would be the best people to approach, but if you can't do that you might talk to a sympathetic teacher or to your doctor. You might be surprised how helpful others can be.

Psychiatric illness

Psychiatric illness can take many forms. It is always unexpected. It can be a minor, shortlived event or it might be more serious. Whatever type of illness it is, it can be a dent to the confidence.

The most usual type of illness is either an anxiety state or a depressive episode. These conditions come out of the blue and they can be very disruptive. The first thing that a sufferer thinks is 'Why me?' Often there is no reason. These things just happen. Fortunately, they are 'self-limiting' conditions, in that they get better of their own accord and in their own time.

The problem is that they leave a hole in your confidence which remains long after they have gone. It takes a long time before one feels secure again and for confidence to return, which it will eventually. You are not the only one to suffer from such a condition. This sort of illness is more common than you think. There is nothing different or odd about you, and other people have regained their confidence and returned to what they were before the illness. You will do just the same, just allow time.

Long illnesses

Any long illness causing a change in your lifestyle or an absence from work can be a problem. Not only do you have to rebuild your strength, but your confidence too. If your problem has been a heart attack or similar condition, it is very important that you rebuild your confidence quickly and fully. You have to get back to living a normal life as soon as possible.

It isn't just confidence in your health that is important. You may find that things have changed at home or at work while you have been away. Someone else may have been taking the decisions, and you may feel that your position has slipped. That can be damaging to your confidence. All that you can do is to set about re-establishing yourself, and you do that by just carrying on as before. You will soon find that you are accepted again.

Unemployment

Finding yourself unemployed, perhaps for the first time in your life, can be a terrible blow to your confidence and your morale. At first you may not be aware of it, but in time it may be your wife who notices that you are not behaving exactly as normal. You may become irritable and uneasy. At first you expect to get a job quickly, and if you are lucky you will. But if there is a delay, applying for jobs becomes more difficult and interviews more of a strain. Your confidence has taken a knock.

Things aren't so bad if you expect some difficulty. You have to cultivate your confidence. You have to work at it by doing the exercises in this book, and by continuing to apply and to go for interviews, even if you have no real expectation of getting the job. Practice and experience always helps.

Harassment

Any kind of continuing harassment will erode your confidence. It may be from a superior at work, constantly criticizing. It may be from obscene phone calls or from the unwelcome attentions of someone you know. Or it might even be from the person to whom you are married. If it goes on long enough it will damage your confidence.

The best way of dealing with this situation is to meet it head on. Confront the person who is causing the trouble before things go too far and your confidence is seriously damaged. Or report the individual to the appropriate authority.

Moving house

This sounds like a simple matter. However, some people think it is one of the most traumatic events we face. It is worse if you go to another town or even another country. You have to start again, make new friends, and start a new life. In this situation, the passage of time helps greatly. But you may well need the help of the exercises and techniques described in this book.

Failure

Any kind of failure is a blow to confidence. It might be failure in examinations, or to gain promotion. There are many kinds of failure.

If you fail at something you have attempted, you have to ask yourself why? You might genuinely not have been well enough prepared. Or you may not have been the best candidate. That's disappointing, but at least your confidence is intact. If you failed because of lack of confidence, then you need the help this book can offer.

Having a baby

This is one of the biggest events in anyone's life. No matter how much one tries to anticipate it, it is always different from what one expects. The feeling of responsibility is overwhelming, and it can make anyone, and perhaps the mother more than the father, feel inadequate. Nature usually has a way of dealing with that, and the duties of motherhood are so onerous that there is no time to think about confidence. The anticipation may be worse than the event.

Bringing up children

Being an adolescent may be trying. Being the parent of one certainly is. It can be very difficult to reconcile yourself to the strains of being the parent of a truculent *almost* grown-up individual. You need all of your self-confidence if you are to survive that.

Divorce

Divorce is always traumatic. There is always a sense of loss, of injustice and of unfulfilled dreams, sometimes bitterness. Divorce is so often acrimonious, but after the event, when things have been settled, one has to pick up the pieces of one's life and carry on. However, maybe many of the friends whom you and your spouse had as a couple will no longer be appropriate for you as a single person. Post-divorce life can be very difficult, and it is very damaging to your confidence.

Again it may not be obvious to you straightaway. It may take time to realise what has happened to your morale. In time you may become aware that some situations are giving you trouble, and you may not know why. The answer may just be that you have lost confidence.

Your confidence may come back as you get used to your new situation. But you may well need some practical help to get you started. Tackle your problem now, using the method I have mentioned.

Bereavement

This is an event which happens to women more than to men. In every marriage there has to be a bereavement, because we don't live forever. It is impossible in a happy marriage for one partner to imagine life without the other, but it does happen, and when it does it is the most traumatic event possible. There is the immediate effect of the grief reaction, and then in the longer term there is the business of constructing a new life without your partner.

If you have been used to a life of shared decisions and of companionship, then there is loneliness. And confidence is lost. Again you can wait all those painful years until you re-establish that confidence, or you can take active steps to rebuild your confidence and your life sooner.

Determination

It is possible to respond to life's events in a passive way, but that isn't very satisfying or successful. You will feel better if you can analyse your problems in detail and set about doing something about them. It does take determination, because none of the techniques I have described are easy. But you now know how to go about solving your problems, and it might well be worth while planning your campaign and making a start now.

But how do you find the confidence to face those special situations that you find particularly difficult? We shall think about that next.

10
Facing a Special Situation

There are things which we all find difficult. Take, for example, appearing on the stage or on radio or television, where we would get "butterflies in the stomach' and other physical sensations. That is normal. Some people find certain situations difficult, maybe those that others would not expect to have problems with. As in many other areas there is no such thing as *normal*.

We are often expected to undertake tasks that we will find difficult, or with which we will have problems – symptoms we get when we are stressed. We have already talked about some of them. We shall now consider how you can deal with these difficult situations.

Preparation

I am going to assume that you have taken the advice offered in earlier chapters and practised your relaxation exercises to a level that will allow you to use them in this difficult situation. It is an important tool to have under your belt. If you haven't been able to do that, here is a tip that might help. If you are in a public place and you start to feel tense, try to go to sleep. If that sounds a little odd, I mean that you should just sit comfortably and relax as if you were going to sleep.

Trying to fall asleep engenders that feeling of relaxation that you have been trying to achieve. It is a short cut, not as good as real relaxation, but good enough in an emergency.

There is no substitute for real preparation. You might ask, 'Why should *I* have to do all this work when others can just stand up and speak off the cuff?' Well, others may not have your particular problems, but then you don't know just how copious the notes on their cuff may be, or how long they have been rehearsing in front of *their* mirror. No, if you are apprehensive, do something about it, and do it early rather than late.

Research

Now is the time to use the methods we have talked about earlier. Find out about your subject, do some research. Ask people what sort of event it is you are going to. You might even visit the location first, so that you are familiar with it when the time comes. Find out who will be there. All this applies as much to a neighbourhood party as to the naming of an ocean liner. You just cannot have too much preparation.

What we are going to do now is to see how we can use the techniques we have learned in particular situations, those for which people seem to need most help.

Medication

Before going any further it is worth saying a few words about medication. I work as a family doctor, so many people expect that I will supply medication as an answer to their immediate problem. I sometimes do this, because there is often not time to pursue the techniques I have described – but these techniques are suitable, and indeed essential, for someone who is lacking in confidence in the long term.

Medication has a limited place in the management of these problems. There are several types of medication that might help, but they should be used with great caution. Some doctors might feel that the use of drugs in this sort of situation is never merited.

If you do feel that you need medication such as tranquillizers, try to start taking it well in advance of the situation you are going to have to face. That will give you time to experience any possible side-effects. The most common of these is drowsiness, and you might find that you really do go to sleep at the event you are going to attend. So drugs are not really the answer. Take them with great caution.

Let us now consider some common situations we may have to face.

Public Speaking

Sooner or later we all have to stand up and make a speech. It might just be a few words, or you might find yourself in a situation where you are expected to make speeches regularly, and this could be a problem.

Speaking in public is just like acting, even if you are acting the part of yourself. The trick is in the preparation. You have to know that if you stand up and your mind goes a blank, you can go on 'auto-pilot' and perform just as well.

That means writing out your speech and possibly learning it off by heart. It means practising it in front of the mirror, recording it on a cassette player and listening to it over and over again. It means learning to slow down your delivery and wait for laughs at your jokes. If you have to tell jokes, try them out on friends first. Everything should be rehearsed and practised.

Have good notes to fall back on. You can't rely on reading a speech, but you need to have something. Notes written on cards are very helpful, but make sure that they are well spaced out with clear underlined headings, so that if you 'dry up' you can find your place easily. You might like to mark different places where you can end your speech if it seems to be too long. You also need to be responsive to the audience. If you want to respond to something which another speaker has said, write it down so that you can refer to it (make sure that you have a pen with you).

If you are giving a lecture, you might consider teaching aids.

Good clear slides or diagrams on the overhead projector can divert your audience and brighten up your presentation. If the audience is happy *you* can relax.

And keep it short. Think of all those tense, phobic people in your audience!

Ceremonies

Weddings, graduation ceremonies and the like can be difficult even if you are only there as a member of the audience. It is the formal atmosphere which is so upsetting. It is deliberately fostered to give the ceremony dignity, which is exactly what is required of an event such as a wedding, or a concert.

At these events you tend to be a passive participant, even if you are involved. Ceremonies are like that. Being passive and quiet can also be a problem, sometimes even more difficult than taking an active part. But you *know* what to expect, so you can use all your confidence-building techniques to help you. As always, it is the anticipation which is worse than the event, so treat it as simply something you have to go through.

Driving Tests

This is a completely different type of event because you have to take an active part. You have to perform well under stress, rather like making a speech or acting in a play.

In this case you will be well rehearsed. Your driving instructor will have made sure of that. He will also have given you tips about the test itself. Yet many people fail the test because they are lacking in confidence. They simply don't do themselves justice, and it is very annoying. Some of course fail because they appear to be overconfident; but that is another matter.

When taking the driving test, one has not only to prepare for the driving part, but also for the ordeal of driving while being critically observed. The only way to do this is to use your imagination. Remember the time when you have done your relaxing, and you sit in a relaxed way and practise difficult situations in your mind? You can do your driving test as often as you want to in the weeks before the actual event itself. And practice makes perfect.

Examinations

As we get older our days of having to take examinations should be over. At least that used to be the case. Nowadays education seems to go on forever and we may still be doing examinations when we are retired. Many retired people already do Open University degrees. It's never too late to start.

Many people feel that they don't do themselves justice because they don't feel confident in examinations. Fortunately, continuous assessment now makes examinations less important. But they still exist.

One word of advice: don't take medication before an examination. You don't want to dull your performance in any way. Prepare as before. Remember that when you are in the examination hall you have more time than you think, so slow down. Take five minutes before you start writing, prepare your mind and actively relax. Then, when you are settled, work steadily and do your best.

Interviews

Interviews can be as stressful as any other event, but it may help if you know what is going on. Some interviews are quite simple and involve only one or two interviewers. They want to find out about you and will ask appropriate questions. You should sit comfortably, relax, take your time and do your best to give honest answers to the questions asked.

Other interviews are not so simple. If it is a serious interview for a promotion or a new job, the interviewing panel may try to provoke you or stress you. They do this by having both a 'nice' and a 'nasty' interviewer. One will ask pleasant questions, and the other will be provocative, and try to unsettle you. That is part of the game. But if you know that you can prepare for it.

Appearing in Court

No one likes appearing in court except lawyers, and they are paid to do it. Courts are designed to be intimidating, and even jury service can be very difficult. All that you can do is to be yourself, but as you know that takes considerable effort, preparation and practice. Courts in real life look just the same as they do on television, but court officials are a little different from their television image.

The judge can be very helpful and the counsel can also encourage you. But as in the interview situation, court can be a game and the opposition lawyer can be fairly objectionable. His task is to disconcert you so that you will appear either an idiot or else unreliable, or both. Remember that everyone in the court, from the judge down, knows the game and what is going on. So just be yourself. Answer honestly and it will be the lawyer who appears bullying or incompetent. There is nothing more disarming than simple honesty.

Travelling

Just being away from home can be disconcerting for some people. For others travelling can be a strain, air travel in particular. And why not? A jet aircraft is an intimidating thing and there is the added difficulty that you can't stop it and get off if you don't like it.

However, flying in a jet is an excellent opportunity for you to practise your relaxation techniques. One thing is certain, if you can actually *get* yourself onto an aircraft you will arrive at the other end. The difficult bit is getting on. So practise at home, during your relaxation sessions. Go to the airport and see what it is like there. There have been recent courses at Teesside Airport simulating air travel for those with flying phobia. Rehearse it in your imagination, but most of all pay your money and *go*.

Sex

I won't dwell on this subject because there are entire books given over to this area. It is worth saying though that the sexual part of our lives is an important and rewarding part, but it is a delicate and sensitive area, so we need confidence if we are to enjoy it and be fulfilled by it.

If you have problems with any part of the business of sex, use the techniques described here, but also seek expert help, or else consult the right books for information and help. The Marriage Guidance Council has an excellent book list, and books can be obtained by mail order.

Now we shall look at the mental attitudes that contribute to our lack of confidence.

11

Knowing Our Mental Attitudes

So far we have talked about positive, practical things that we can do to improve our confidence. We have steered clear of any gratuitous advice about how we should think, for the very good reason that we know that we cannot control our thoughts. We can try to *think* positively, but it is much more constructive to try to *act* positively. We know we can achieve this no matter how self-conscious or uncomfortable we may feel. We can train ourselves to overcome these feelings.

However, we *can* look critically at some aspects of our approach to life.

Our attitude to ourselves

A few years ago we heard a lot about people with *inferiority complexes*. It seemed to be fashionable to describe oneself or others in that way, without perhaps knowing exactly what was meant by the term. Maybe they just meant that they felt inferior to some other people.

That would not be strange, because we all feel inferior to someone. There has to be a 'top dog' – some individuals have a natural authority and we defer to them. It is a matter of degree, like almost any other psychological problem. But if you feel inferior to *everyone* then you have a real problem. However, nobody feels inferior to everyone. We have some idea of our own value if we are strictly honest. The problem is that it isn't as easy as it seems to achieve that strictly honest view.

Looking at ourselves

Psychologists have shown that some of us have a distorted image of ourselves. That is to say that though we may form an honest opinion of our own worth, it is the wrong opinion. We are actually better, more competent, more socially aware and in every way better than we *think* we are. So we think of ourselves as being inferior, but in fact we are not at all. Why does this happen?

It might just be this business of learning the wrong lessons as we go through life, from some unfortunate experiences. Some thing which is unsatisfactory for some quite independent reason may make you feel that it is your fault in some way. That makes you cautious, and on the next similar occasion you make the same assumption. So over the years your opinion of your own worth becomes distorted.

It might of course be that you have something to gain from playing the part of someone who is less competent than he or she really is. Believing that saves you from having to make an effort. Or you may be one of those people who gets symptoms in certain situations, so you solve that problem for yourself by just saying, 'There's no point in me trying to do that. I'm just not as good as other people are. Let *them* get on with it.'

You may strike this attitude subconsciously without being aware of it at all. But remember our promise to ourselves that we would be strictly honest? Now is the time to honour that promise.

What are we capable of doing

How can we decide what we are capable of doing, or what our true worth really is? It isn't easy to reorganize our thinking in this way, but we have to do it. The alternative is to go through life with a distorted view of ourselves, which will stop us from doing many of the things we could and should be doing. It might even stop us from meeting and forming a normal relationship with the sort of person we might want to eventually marry. Or hold us back from seeking a promotion at work, so that we never fulfil our true potential. All of these things would be sad because they are avoidable. But how are they to be avoided?

We have agreed that society has a natural hierarchy, and that we all have a place in that order of things somewhere.

But some of us underestimate our worth. Others overestimate it and push themselves forward. They may have problems, but these will not be problems of underconfidence and they will not be reading this book. They may be successful people in many ways, but they will not be well liked and in the end they may not be as successful as you will be when you have overcome your problems.

So we are trying to find a way of gaining insight into our position, trying to look into ourselves and to compare what we find there with others.

Making comparisons

We need to sit down with our pencil and paper again, and make a few lists. First of all, how about a list of the people around you, those with whom you work, or know socially? The list should include both sexes, as for these purposes we can compare ourselves with the opposite sex as well as with our own.

Now we need a list of what we consider to be important attributes, that matter in our opinion. You might start with physical appearance, then sense of humour, ability to get on with others, consideration to others, ability to explain difficult ideas.

The list can be long or short. Include as many items as you can, as personal as you like. The personal things may be the most important.

Now give every person on your list a score out of ten for each item. If you have ten items then each person will have a score out of 100. Take your time and make it as accurate as you can.

Then, add your name to the bottom of the list and give yourself a score just like the others. No-one is going to see it apart from you, so you can afford to be as honest as you like. How does your score compare to the others? My guess is that you may not be the worst. You might even do quite well.

But what if you don't do well? Can you afford to take that chance? Of course you can. If you find certain items on which you don't score well, then you know what you are going to have to work on. You can only win at this exercise.

The point of the operation is to get to know your real self. You have to become comfortable with what you are, and to fulfil your real potential unhindered by self-doubt.

'Decatastrophizing' situations

This may be one of the most important items in this book, and the most enjoyable, and perhaps the most helpful. So what do we mean by 'decatastrophizing?'

Everyone who lacks confidence says to himself at some time, 'What would happen if. . .?' What would happen if I dried up in the middle of a speech; if I asked this girl out and she refused to come; if I fainted; if I couldn't breathe and I had to leave the meeting; if I said something stupid and everyone laughed?

The answer to all these questions is *nothing*.

Imaginative people tend to worry too much about the consequences of their actions. Everything is a potential catastrophe. Nothing can be allowed to go wrong, they must never get themselves into a situation which might cause even the slightest embarrassment. So if you think, for example,

'What would happen if I dried up in the middle of a speech,' you should ask yourself 'Right, what *would* happen?'

There might be a brief pause while you looked at your notes. You might want to take a drink of water. One or two people might think, 'He's lost his place,' but most wouldn't even notice, and if they did you would still be alive and at your work in the morning.

What would happen if you asked a girl out and she refused? You'd just have to ask someone else, wouldn't you? It literally wouldn't be the end of the world. It wouldn't be a catastrophe.

So next time you are worried about some event, ask yourself 'What would happen if. . .?' But this time answer the question, what *would* happen? And keep asking the question. What would happen if I had to leave a meeting? If your answer is that everyone would notice and wonder why, then ask yourself what would happen if they did wonder why? They might think that you were ill. What would happen if they thought you were ill? And again, the answer is that people often feel ill, so they might just assume that it was too hot or that you had eaten too much lunch.

Keep asking the question. Get angry with it. Shout at yourself a bit. Keep seeking the consequences of any supposed catatrophe until even you are certain that there would be no catastrophe after all. It *is* possible to de-catastrophize any situation. Nothing is that important.

How is your confidence faring now? Let us consider what we have achieved.

12

What Have We Achieved?

What we have been saying about improving our confidence has been based on our knowledge of certainties, not on theoretical ideas. We know that confidence *can* be improved. We know that it takes time and commitment. We know that we have the time, but have we got the commitment?

We have been talking about such things as doing exercises with pencil and paper, or relaxation exercises. We have been talking about preparing in advance for events that others might take as a matter of course. We have been talking about physical fitness, and about working harder than anyone else.

No-one said it would be easy. But we did say that it would work. Only *you* can decide whether it is worth the effort or not. Now you know that it can be done, as it has been done before. So if you decide not to tackle your problem, at least you know what you are missing.

There are very few people who would not make a substantial effort to improve their self-confidence. Lacking confidence is such a huge drawback that most people would do anything to improve it. But there are practical difficulties to be overcome, and they should not be underestimated. It is more difficult than you think. It is easy to talk about a problem, but much more difficult to put the ideas into practice.

You will have to make a big effort. It takes time, and there are always demands on our time. There is always a temptation to back-slide, to miss a day's relaxation exercises because there is something important on television. And there are disappointments and bad days when nothing seems to go right.

You just have to keep at it. If you have someone to help you then you are lucky. It is hard to do these things on your own.

73

You really do need encouragement. If you are married, or have someone close to you, he or she may help you. However, be careful about discussing your problems with just anyone. Many people don't understand, or perhaps pretend not to understand because they feel threatened by the possible exposure of their own lack of confidence.

But why should other people have it so easy? Or do they actually have it so easy? Remember that I am a general practitioner and I see a lot of patients every day. They all have problems of some sort, many of them the same as yours. No one is immune, not even the great and the good.

A friend of mine was sitting on the platform at a political meeting at which a former prime minister was to speak. She suddenly noticed that he was shaking from head to foot. As soon as he got up to speak, he settled down, but he experienced the same 'butterflies' as you do. Many entertainers have the same problem, and they have to work to overcome their difficulties. In this life no-one is what they seem, we all put on an act. But be honest with *yourself*. You can fool others, but you must *never* fool yourself.

What I have described here is an approach to your problem. Don't feel the need to adhere to it rigidly. Don't cut corners, but you can add ideas of your own if you think they will be more appropriate to your particular problem. Don't be afraid to experiment; you know what you are trying to achieve and you can work out ways of doing that.

Remember to proceed in easy stages. Don't be too ambitious too soon, because you will be disappointed. Take it easy. You have plenty of time, use it initially to think about your problem and let your ideas mature. Then you can let your ingenuity take its course.

Remember also that nothing is fixed in this life. Confidence improves as you get older, unless some life event occurs which sets you back. A 35-year-old woman is never put upon by shop assistants in the way a 20-year-old woman might be. And getting married or buying a house, or any one of many such events can improve your confidence. But you cannot afford to wait for fate to help you. God helps those who help themselves.

Once you've made a start on your problem you may be surprised at what happens. Confidence inspires confidence, and your relationships with others may improve dramatically.

But if something does happen to dent your self-confidence, don't panic. You don't ever go back to the beginning again. All that you have learned about yourself remains, and self-knowledge is the key to progress. You will quickly get back on your feet again.

Only seek to change your confidence. You can't change your personality, you are born with that and stuck with it. You might need to develop the confidence to let attributes such as kindness and consideration show. Underconfident people sometimes put up barriers so successfully that they appear to be hard and uncaring. Have the confidence to let your emotions show.

Learn to trust people. Most people are trustworthy and dependable and they want the same kind of caring as you do. It is better to trust some people and to be occasionally disappointed than never to trust anyone at all. That is a bleak prospect.

You have everything to gain and absolutely nothing to lose. Why should you accept life as it is if that life can be improved? The practical exercises in this book will help you to be yourself. But they can do no more than that. *You* have to supply the commitment, and dare I say it, the courage. It isn't easy to hazard a fragile personality in a dangerous world.

However, it is a world full of rich experiences, and if you are missing any of those experiences then you must make every effort to improve your confidence. Make the decision to start. Then just get on with it. Life is there to be lived. You only have one chance.

Good luck.

Index

Dr Kenneth Hambly

THE NERVOUS PERSON'S COMPANION

A reassuring friend at your side, to help you build up your self-confidence bit by bit, until you can do whatever you like, without being held back by your nerves.
£4·99

OVERCOMING TENSION

Simple questionnaires, helpful advice and a proven method to help you overcome tension, anxiety and phobias without taking tranquillisers.
£4·99